The Donut That Roared!

By Joan Yordy Brasher
with Jackson Grant

Have you ever heard
a donut

roar

I have —
many times before.

I've witnessed all
its loudmouthed glory,
but that's just
one part of my story.

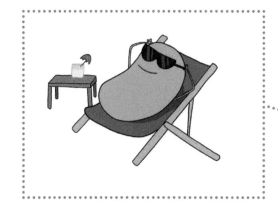

A jelly bean
is in my brain,
and sometimes
it can be a pain.

So doctors photograph the bean

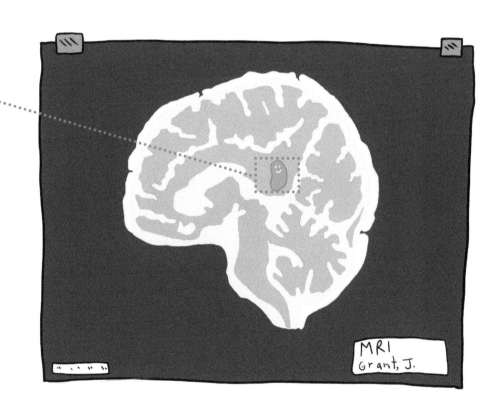

MRI
Grant, J.

with a great big noisy
donut machine!

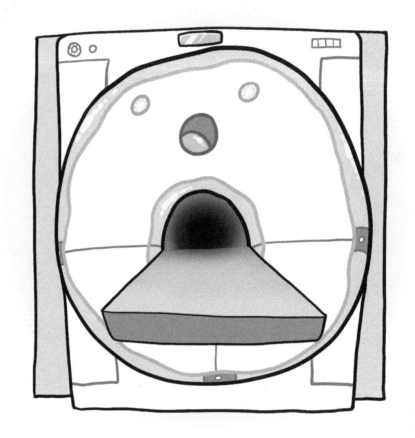

At first I was nervous—
well, wouldn't you be?
But soon it was easy as 1-2-3!

I always wear my favorite socks.
And holding Lamby helps a lot.

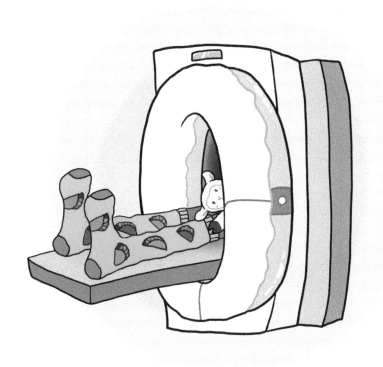

The donut doesn't hurt a bit.
I slide right in, a perfect fit.

And then the donut
starts to roar
just like so many
times before.

roarrrr

roarrrr

roarrrr

roarrrr

roarrrr

roarrrr

roarrrr

roarrrr

roarrrr

roarrr roarrr roarrr roarrr roarrr roarrr roarrr roarrr roarrr roarrr roarrr roar

I close my eyes,
try not to worry.

'Cuz squirming
makes the pictures

BLURRY.

I tell myself, Don't wiggle about.

Breathe in,

breathe out.

Breathe in,

breathe out.

Just when it gets
extreeeeeeeeemely boring

The donut finally stops
its roaring.

roarrrr

roarrrr

roarrrr

roarrrr

roarrrr

roarrrr

roarrrr

roarrrr

roarrrr

Another scan is
done at last.
It's time to do
my happy dance!

My friend from Child
Life gives high fives.
And then my family
all arrives.

Waiting for me is my mother,
my dad, my auntie and my brother.

We always go for chili fries
to celebrate my MRIs.

So many scans,
I've lost count of them.

And now
that donut
is a friend.

Its pictures help
my doctors know
just how to help
me heal and grow.

So if you need a scan
(or three),
It's not so bad—
just wait and see.

Relax, breathe deep
and do your best

And let the donut do the rest.

A LETTER FROM JACKSON GRANT

PHOTO BY JOHN LUCAS

Dear friend,

When I was 10 years old, I was diagnosed with a benign brain tumor the size of a jelly bean. The first thing I had to do was get an MRI because my doctor needed to make sure my brain was growing properly. That was the first of many MRIs. In the beginning, I was pretty nervous because I didn't know what to expect. The MRI machine is really noisy! So I decided to use my imagination to come up with ways to make my MRIs less stressful.

One day I saw a little boy and his mom come in to the waiting area. The boy looked really scared and I realized it was his first MRI. I felt so sad and wished there was something I could do to help him see that he really could do it. At that moment I started to imagine creating a book that could help children everywhere feel better about their MRI experience. My Aunt Joan helped me create this book, and we hope it helps you and your whole family.

JEAN, ISAIAH, JACKSON AND RUPERT

I still get MRIs every few months, but it's not as scary for me as it used to be. It's just a small part of my life, and it doesn't slow me down. I play soccer, ride my bike and shoot hoops with my brother and our friends. I even went on an extreme sports adventure in New Zealand (Thank you Make-A-Wish Los Angeles!), where I got to bungee-jump!

You may have noticed there are journaling pages at the end of the book. When I first found out I had a brain tumor, I started writing in my journal about it and it helped me figure out how I was feeling. I hope you will write down your thoughts and feelings, as well as your own tricks and tips for getting through an MRI.

The main thing to remember is that you are not alone, and you are much stronger than you know!

Love,
Jackson

Follow me on Instagram at @donutthatroared and share your MRI story.

PHOTOS BY
AMY WENDLING

FREQUENTLY ASKED QUESTIONS

ANSWERED BY CHILD LIFE SPECIALISTS

What is a Magnetic Resonance Imaging (MRI) scanner?

An MRI scanner is a huge donut-shaped machine. It uses high-tech magnetic fields and radio waves to create detailed images of the inside of your body. It's like an X-ray machine but even more precise. Because of the magnetic fields, you cannot bring anything metal into the MRI room.

Why is the MRI machine so noisy?

It's very scientific. In order to create the detailed scans, rapid pulses of electricity are pushed through metal coils, causing a variety of roaring and banging sounds. These sounds may be as loud as 125 decibels, which is equivalent to a rock concert or a balloon popping near the ear! That is why ear protection is provided.

How does getting an MRI work?

When you arrive you may get to pick out a movie to watch while you are in the scanner. You will be given headphones to protect your ears as well as a button to push if you need to speak to the tech during the scan. Some children say it feels like they are astronauts inside of a space ship! A parent can usually stay in the room with you. The most important thing is to remain very still during the MRI and just try to ignore all the loud noises. Practicing at home ahead of time may help.

Does it hurt?

An MRI does not hurt. The only thing that might be a bit ouchy is if you have to get a contrast IV, which helps make the photos even more detailed. There is a little pinch when they put it in. But the noisy donut-shaped machine will not hurt you.

How long does an MRI take?

Each one is different. Some take 10 minutes, while others can take longer, like an hour or more.

Can I bring my favorite stuffed animal?

You can usually bring a small stuffed animal or a blanket in the scanner.

What does a Child Life Specialist do?

Hospitals have Child Life Specialists to answer your questions, help you find ways to deal with stress or anxiety and keep you company. They can help make your hospital experience less scary for you and your whole family. Learn more at **child-life.org**.

31

Jackson's MRI Tips

When I found out I was going to be getting MRIs every few months, I decided to come up with creative ways to make my MRI day easier. I was 10 so I wanted it to be fun — not scary or hard. I hope these will help you too.

Wear comfy clothes like sweats, a favorite soft t-shirt, even your jammies! I love to wear my taco socks! The room may be cold, but inside the MRI machine it is toasty warm.

Take something special with you, like a small stuffed animal or toy (I always take my Lamby!). As long as it doesn't have metal in it, you can take it into the MRI machine with you.

Use your imagination! Every time I go into the MRI machine, **I imagine I am a different flavor of donut** — chocolate, raspberry or cream-filled. Sometimes I imagine sprinkles! What is your favorite kind of donut?

If you have to get an IV, **tell your doctor or Child Life Specialist to help distract you with a book or funny video.** Sometimes I focus on a dot on the wall, or imagine what I am going to do after the MRI.

When it's time for my MRI, **I prepare myself by imagining myself being very calm and relaxed** in the MRI machine. I try to relax and breathe softly, visualizing a positive experience.

I like to plan something fun for after the MRI, like play a game when I get home, visit a friend, or have lunch with my family. I like to go for chili fries afterward, but sometimes my mom makes me eat something healthy instead!

Being nervous is super normal. **I decided that I was going to be EXCITED instead of nervous.** I began to see my MRIs as an adventure!

Use your voice! If you are nervous, talk to your family, your doctor and your friends for support. You are not alone, and soon you will be a pro at getting an MRI, just like me!

Order copies of this book at
donutthatroared.com

Contact Us:

EMAIL: donutthatroared@gmail.com
FACEBOOK: @donutthatroared
INSTAGRAM: @donutthatroared

ABOUT THE AUTHOR
Joan Yordy Brasher is Jackson's aunt.
She is a writer, editor and artist, and
lives in Nashville, Tennessee.

my MRI journal

my MRI journal

CPSIA information can be obtained
at www.ICGtesting.com
Printed in the USA
LVHW071136030320
648824LV00033B/510